Getting in Touch with your Inner Bitch

ELIZABETH HILTS

SOURCEBOOKS HYSTERIA®
AN IMPRINT OF SOURCEBOOKS, INC.®
NAPERVILLE, ILLINOIS

Copyright © 2006 by Elizabeth Hilts
Cover and internal design © 2006 by Sourcebooks, Inc.
Cover photo © Stephanie Piro
Cartoons © Nicole Hollander, Marian Henley, Mary Lawton and Stephanie Piro
Sourcebooks and the colophon are registered trademarks of Sourcebooks, Inc.

All rights reserved. No part of this book may be reproduced in any form or by any electronic or mechanical means including information storage and retrieval systems—except in the case of brief quotations embodied in critical articles or reviews—without permission in writing from its publisher, Sourcebooks, Inc.

Published by Sourcebooks Hysteria, an imprint of Sourcebooks, Inc.
P.O. Box 4410, Naperville, Illinois 60567–4410
(630) 961-3900
Fax: (630) 961-2168
www.sourcebooks.com
ISBN-13: 978-1-4022-07952
ISBN-10: 1-4022-07956

Library of Congress Cataloging-in-Publication Data

Hilts, Elizabeth.
  Getting in touch with your inner bitch / by Elizabeth Hilts. -- 3rd ed.
      p. cm.
  ISBN-13: 978-1-4022-0771-6
  ISBN-10: 1-4022-0771-9
  1. Women--Humor. I. Title.

Printed and bound in United States
VP 10 9 8 7 6

Dedication

This book is for my daughter, Shannon Hillory Hector, whose insight and assistance were essential elements in its completion, my granddaughter, Cassidy Elizabeth Singleton, who is continuing the fine family tradition of being a strong female, my husband, Neil Swanson, for being my safe harbor and for making me laugh more (and harder) than any other human being, and for my father, Robert Gifford Hilts, whom I still miss every day.

Acknowledgments

I would like to offer special thanks to the women who keep me honest, provide the support I need to continue discovering the power of my Inner Bitch, and make me laugh out loud: Dawn Collins, Laura Fedele, Aida Little, Elaine Osowski, Ingrida Perri, and Felicia Moreland Robinson.

Thank you to all the people who played a part in making this book happen in the first place: Jim Motavalli (who believed in me long before I believed in myself); Mary Ann Masarech; Judith Gardner; Karen Drena; Piper Machette; Richard Howe; my fairy godmother, Jocelyn K. Moreland; David Robinson; Jeff Yoder; and Mace Norwood, who was right all those years ago.

My agent, Tom Connor, provided invaluable guidance and clarity in the process of finding a home for the Inner Bitch. It continues to be a pleasure to share this adventure with him.

Thanks to Sarah Waite and Lysbeth Guillorn for research and editing the first edition and to Susie Benton for her assistance with this version; to the incomparable Nicole Hollander for creating the original cover and, along with Marian Henley and Mary Lawton, the cartoons that still illustrate the absurdities of women's everyday lives.

Very special thanks to Deborah Werksman for her insistence on bringing the Inner Bitch to the world.

And a big shout out to all the women and men who "get" the Inner Bitch.

Contents

"Do what you feel in your heart to be right—for you'll be criticized anyway. You'll be damned if you do, and damned if you don't."

—Eleanor Roosevelt

Introduction
Stood Up; Wised Up

L et me take a few moments to explain why I wrote this book.

It started many years ago in February 1993 with my article, "Get in Touch with Your Inner Bitch," published in *Hysteria*, the humor magazine for women.

The magazine came out, a radio personality saw the article and called me for an interview, and suddenly I was deemed the Expert on the Inner Bitch.

Well, I am. But before I became the Expert on Her, I was an expert on the topic of Toxic Niceness. I was trained from the day of my birth in the ways of being Nice. The first thing my mother ever said to me was, "Elizabeth, behave."

And I tried. Honestly. I attempted to be a paragon of Niceness—a Melanie Wilkes, a Beth (from *Little Women*—or was it Amy?), a Nancy Drew. I memorized the names of the most toxic family, the Nicelys—Act,

Speak, Sit, Think, even Dress. I was, however, not very good at any of this.

> *"A young lady is a female child who has just done something dreadful."*
>
> —Judith Martin

Speak Nicely was tough. I tried to keep my voice low and well modulated. When that didn't work, I pushed it a full octave higher, which forced me to whisper. I thought I sounded sweet. Everyone else thought I had laryngitis.

Dress Nicely nearly pushed me to the edge. The first clue that this goal was going to prove problematic involved those little anklet socks with lace trim—which trim inevitably ended up creeping down into my Mary Janes and lodging in a tattered, mysteriously grimy mass under my heel. Not the neat, well-turned out effect my mother hoped for and which my peers pulled off with no tugging, yanking, or discernable effort whatsoever. Add in my flyaway hair, my tendency to get banged up while indulging in my passion for climbing trees, plus my heartfelt desire to wear jeans and a t-shirt whenever possible and the result fell far short of the Dress Nicely goal. When I began blossoming into womanhood it was even more challenging. Dress Nicely, when I wanted halter tops. Décolletage (non-existent, in my case)! Spandex!

"Remember that always dressing in understated good taste is the same as playing dead."

—Susan Catherine

But in the end, it was old Act Nicely that was the most toxic of the Nicelys for me. There was so much pressure to "behave"—which was code for putting on a pleasing demeanor. Not just from the adults in my life—who I'm certain believed they had my best interests in mind—but also from my girl friends.

*"She was a perfect lady—
just set in her seat and stared."*

—**Eudora Welty**

It's somewhat alarming to remember how many of my female friends were prone to sudden outbursts of the most damaging slogan for Toxic Niceness in existence—"Sugar and spice and everything NICE, that's what little girls are made of"—at the oddest moments. For instance, when I was pressing my case for a rousing game of touch football instead of going inside to play with their "Dolls of Many Lands" collection, the girls I knew would put their little hands on their hips, sashay up to well within spitting range, and hiss those thirteen words in a menacing sing-song. It wasn't much of an argument, really. Nor were they exhibiting the niceness they advocated. "Nice," as was so often the case, meant acquiescence and it was clear that my next move was capitulation. I'd follow them inside where the "play" consisted mostly of gazing in mute admiration at impossibly statuesque and glamorous icons of womanhood while trying to ignore the gleeful hoots and hollers of the neighborhood lads.

At the same time I noticed that those same boys seemed to have a built-in excuse for acting in ways that didn't fit into any definition of nice. You may have heard this magic phrase—"boys will be boys." It was almost enough to make a person want to be one. A boy, I mean. Except that, well...

"I didn't want to be a boy, ever, but I was outraged that his height and intelligence were graces for him and gaucheries for me."

—Jane Rule

It got even worse as we progressed to our preteen years. Along with the onslaught of puberty came a veritable tidal wave of advice on the best way to catch a boy. Never mind that the objects of all that energy were relatively oblivious to our wiles. Or that, frankly, the pool of potential Prince Charmings were, for the most part, anything but charming. Our entire focus was on interpreting the behavior of this exotic species and applying a scholarly approach to the best methods for capturing their attention and adoration.

"I got desperate and went to one of those expensive matchmakers. She was so romantic: 'You've got to get a guy on the hook. You reel him in slowly.' I asked, 'When do I fillet him?' I don't know much more about relationships, but I can run a fish and chips shop."

—Maura Kennedy

While there were many mysteries inherent in attaining the coveted role of "someone's girlfriend," the consensus seemed to be that "being nice" was vital. "Nice" seemed to have taken on the added dimension of playing dumb, which manifested itself in giggling at nearly every word a boy said. Not laughing, giggling. It went without saying that challenging boys in any way—on the playing field (which we studiously avoided), in the classroom, when they made some ridiculous statement—was completely forbidden. At the same time, there was an almost intuitive understanding that one could be too nice, which apparently had something to do with not opening one's mouth during a kiss.

At that point my training took on a whole new level of intensity. When I laughed too loud, when I actually said the things I knew we were all thinking, my girlfriends would say, "Stop making a spectacle of yourself!"

If extreme discretion was called for, they would nudge my arm and hiss, "Liiiiiz!" It almost made me long for the old "Dolls of Many Lands" days.

*"The Word 'Lady':
Most Often Used to Describe
Someone You Wouldn't Want
to Talk to for Even Five Minutes."*

—**Fran Lebowitz**

In private, they shrieked with laughter as they recounted the story of my latest outrageous behavior.

All the while, however, lurking just under the anxious surface of niceness was our awareness of a basic, fearsome truth: It was the bitches who got all the good stuff.

> *"I love to see a young girl go out and grab the world by the lapels. Life's a bitch. You've got to go out and kick ass."*
>
> —Maya Angelou

I mean, Scarlett O'Hara was the star of the movie, wasn't she? And she got the sequel. Melanie may have had Ashley, but who wanted Ashley? Anyone with eyes could see that Ashley was—Ashley.

But I continued to try to force myself inside a sort of Niceness suit in hopes that someday it would prove to be a comfortable fit. Eventually, I manifested all the Niceness I could, bending over backwards to be agreeable, helpful, thoughtful, adoring, and adorable—in other words, a complete doormat.

Until IT happened. The event that finally made me see that Niceness could be toxic.

The Moment of Truth

IT had to do with a man. In my case, that phrase can be followed with thc addendum, "of course." I used to find this an acutely embarrassing story, but that was before I really understood how debilitating the effects of Toxic Niceness are and how important sharing these experiences is in overcoming this epidemic. Here's what happened: I got stood up.

Yes. Left sitting in my living room on a Saturday night. After I'd tried on and rejected five different (fabulous) outfits. I called his house, got his machine. Left a message. "Hi, It's nearly nine o'clock. You must be running late. See you when you get here." Nine-Fifteen, nine forty-five. I went upstairs at ten-thirty, took off my makeup, and got into bed, where I spent a sleepless night, tossing and turning from concern to anger and back again all night.

"Maybe he had an accident?" I worried.

"He better have broken his jaw and both hands, complicated by total amnesia," a little voice inside my head responded.

"Oh. My. God! He could be lying in a ditch some-where! Maybe I should go look for him."

"Maybe you'd better figure out once and for all if it's 'lying' in a ditch or just plain 'lying'—which seems like a better use of your time and energy. He's a lying liar is what he is. Forget him!"

He called the next day and actually said, "Something came up. You understand, don't you?"

Of course I did. I understood completely. He had a better offer and she was, undoubtedly, so much nicer—or something—than I ever could be. But I forgave him anyway because he was really cute, and I really liked him. Mostly, however, because no one likes a bitch. How could a nice girl like me stay angry? He asked for another chance and I gave it to him.

> *"If you always do what you always did, you'll always get what you always got."*
>
> —Anonymous

You know it had to happen again. And this time, I went ballistic! I called his answering machine, ranting and raving until the tape ran out. Then I called back to yell some more. Finally, on the third go-round, I was all yelled out and the old training kicked in. "I'm really sorry, but I am really hurt," I whispered hoarsely into the phone. "Please call me."

Now that's embarrassing! I can't believe it myself. I apologized! I told his answering machine I was hurt! I wasn't hurt, I was furious! But, you know, he was cute, and I thought I could, maybe, really like him, and he'd never treat me so badly if he knew how nice I could be.

There's a world of difference between "being nice" and "being Nice." That Nice thing always bites us in the ass.

Right. The truth is, he'd never have treated me so badly if he knew what a bitch I could be. If I had been in touch with my Inner Bitch at that point, I would have called him on his disrespectful shenanigans immediately. I certainly wouldn't have spent an entire night wondering what failing on my part could have explained his complete lack of common courtesy and I never would have given him a second chance.

However, it took this incident to get me in touch with my Inner Bitch, and when I realized what I'd done, I decided right then and there that it was time to give up Toxic Niceness. It was time to emulate the bitches of the world. I would, as my mother would say, take a page from their book.

But there was no book.

Until now.

My daughter has a T-shirt that reads, "If you think I'm a bitch, you should meet my mother." I'm so proud...

"No woman is all sweetness."

—Mme. Récamier

Chapter One
Toxic Niceness

*W*hat is this mysterious malady that drives us to self-defeating behavior? Some people call this syndrome by different names: the "disease to please," co-dependency, nurturing. Your Inner Bitch wants you to consider that "nurturing" may just be Toxic Niceness in wolf's clothing.

When we suffer from Toxic Niceness, we work hard to make things a little sweeter. Far too often, this is achieved at a terrible cost to ourselves.

After a while Toxic Niceness begins to feel like that slightly too-tight pair of jeans we sometimes insist on wearing—it might look great to everyone else, but it's hard to sit in for an entire day.

The bottom line is this: When we suffer from Toxic Niceness, everyone else in our lives gets more out of our efforts than we do. Toxic Niceness leads us to think things like, "Eventually we'll do what I want to do." The Inner Bitch, on the other hand, leads us to say things like, "I'll visit your family this weekend, but next weekend we're going antiquing."

Our Families

"If you only try to please others, you're going to resent those people you're trying to please, the ones who are often closest to you. If you choose a path that you yourself want to take, then you're going to be much kinder to the people in your life."

—Sarah McLachlan

Our menfolk get to actually relax after work and on weekends while we take care of the laundry, the housekeeping, the grocery shopping, and the thousand and one little things that have to be done to ensure that some degree of order can be maintained.

Our children get all of those benefits plus chauffeur services, tutoring, a live-in personal assistant who makes sure that the library books are returned on time, and every conceivable craft supply they might need for school projects is in stock.

Your Inner Bitch understands that guilt—while it is the gift that keeps on giving—is a useless emotion. Move on. Your Inner Bitch doesn't believe in the myth of "happily ever after" any more than she believes that Toxic Niceness is a good thing.

Our Friends

"The emotional, sexual, and psychological stereotyping of females begins when the doctor says, 'It's a girl.'"

—Shirley Chisholm

Our friends get a shoulder to cry on, a sympathetic ear, assistance with thankless tasks like pet-sitting, closet clearing, and the removal of the mountain of belongings left behind by a recently absconding ex.

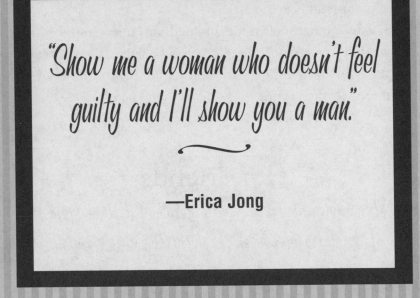

"Show me a woman who doesn't feel guilty and I'll show you a man."

—Erica Jong

Your Inner Bitch knows that when faced
with a situation that kicks you into High Toxicity,
it's time to call a friend who can coach you out of it.

Our Coworkers

"If you're saddled by the need to know the outcome
before you set out, you limit your possibilities."

—Janet Carlson Freed

Our co-workers get someone who can be relied on to pick up an endless supply of slack so they can actually leave at 5:30 every night. Our employers get a dedicated worker who always gives 110 percent without asking for as much as a cost-of-living increase. Our direct reports get someone to take on all the effort involved in meeting demands for increased productivity without increased resources.

An Inner Bitch Reminder:

If you don't say what it is you want,
you'll never get it. This applies equally
to raises, fair play, your partner's
attention, and active participation
in housework, a foot rub...
the list goes on and on.

None of this is terrible and much of it is actually quite fulfilling. Except that Toxic Niceness is, by definition, a good thing taken to the extreme. And it creates something of a double-bind for those of us who suffer from it. We are making lemonade out of life's lemon, using our own personal sugar.

> *"Nobody's interested in sweetness and light."*
> —Hedda Hopper

When we live with Toxic Niceness, we live on the giving end of a one-way street. Even when offers of reciprocation are made, those of us who suffer from Toxic Niceness feel honor-bound to refuse them. The Toxic Niceness definition of teamwork is "get along." The Inner Bitch knows that teamwork requires careful assessment of each situation and speaking out about problems and issues. Your Inner Bitch wants you to consider this: If life seems like a constant déjà vu, apply a simple "I don't think so" to those situations that aren't working for you.

Toxic Niceness has an expiration date.
Act accordingly at the beginning of every relationship,
with friends, with men, and at work.

The Signs

"I always wanted to be somebody, but now I realize
I should have been more specific."

—Lily Tomlin

The fact that you are reading this is proof that you are willing to consider letting go of Toxic Niceness. Are you a long-time sufferer of the syndrome? Ask yourself these questions:

1. Have you ever wanted to give someone a piece of your mind and eaten a piece of cake instead?
2. How about the whole cake?
3. Have the words, "I don't know what came over me!" ever sprung from your lips?

4. Have you ever refused an invitation because you were hoping that your latest love interest would finally ask you out on Saturday night?
5. Have you ever sat at home alone on Saturday night because he never called?
6. Have you ever said "yes" when you meant "I don't think so"?
7. Do you apologize for walking into someone else's office to ask a perfectly legitimate business-related question?
8. Have you ever worn a bridesmaid's dress with spaghetti straps?

If you answered yes to any of these questions, it's a sure thing that you're using too much sugar. But all is not lost—take heart. Toxic Niceness need not be a problem any longer.

Live at the Edge

"When in doubt, make a fool of yourself. There is a microscopically thin line between being brilliantly creative and acting like the most gigantic idiot on earth. So what the hell, leap."

—Cynthia Heimel

If you're wondering whether it's a good day to be in touch with your Inner Bitch, remember this: she is the little black dress of attitudes, perfect for every occasion. Slipping into Toxic Niceness? Just ask yourself if you really want to ever wear (and pay for) another taffeta bridesmaid's dress with spaghetti straps. That'll help.

Being in touch with your Inner Bitch means never having to say, "I don't know what came over me." You know, and you're not afraid to say so.

Don't Just Sit There

"There have been women in the past far more daring than we would need to be now, who ventured all and gained a little, but survived after all."

—Germaine Greer

Your Inner Bitch knows that power is at our feet. Or maybe on our desks. Another good reason to get rid of clutter.

Your Inner Bitch knows when to be firm, when to state a position, and how to act upon her convictions.

On a serious note, the roots of Toxic Niceness are based in a belief that everything is our fault, that we can never really be nice enough, or pretty enough, or that we don't deserve anything good. Which is a terrible way to live. Toxic Niceness may be an effective way to get what you want, if what you want is endless frustration and a nagging feeling that there's got to be something more in life.

Have you ever worn
a foam green bridesmaid's dress
with spaghetti straps?
That was brought about
by Toxic Niceness.

Remember: being in touch with your
Inner Bitch means never wearing
taffeta again.

Take a sip of water before you say "yes" to yet another drain on your precious internal resources. Your Inner Bitch wants to remind you to hydrate often, and remember how refreshing a good "I don't think so" can be.

Cast off the mantle of Toxic Niceness and acknowledge that powerful and integral part of each of us known as the Inner Bitch. Don't pretend you don't know what I'm talking about. No one can maintain Toxic Niceness for an entire lifetime. Eventually it's going to end in the nastiest of ways: either you'll melt into a pool of sugar or you'll explode in a torrent of invectives. Why not choose the Inner Bitch instead?

One benefit of giving up Toxic Niceness is that we approach every relationship—with friends, with family, in business, and in romance—sure of our status as equals.

Toxic Niceness asks, "Do you like me?"
The Inner Bitch asks, "Do I like you?"

Read on. Your Inner Bitch awaits you.

SYLVIA
by Nicole Hollander

To paraphrase the African proverb:
"The best time to have gotten in touch
with your Inner Bitch was
twenty years ago.
The second best time is now."

Chapter Two
Meet Your Inner Bitch

Finding the Bitch Within

Remember, "Nice" is a four-letter word.

There is a powerful and integral part of each of us that has until now gone unrecognized, its energy largely untapped. Years of repression have sent this aspect of our selves into hiding in the nooks and crannies of our souls. Because we misunderstand it, we do all we can to keep it in the dark where we believe it belongs.

It is the Inner Bitch. Don't pretend you don't know what I'm talking about.

"Take care to get what you like or you will be forced to like what you get."

—George Bernard Shaw

We all know Her. She floats constantly just under the surface of our consciousness and our culture. She is a part of ourselves that is smart, confident, dignified, and knows what she wants. She tells us not to settle for less. The Inner Bitch is like an early warning system in the battle for self-esteem and dignity, alerting us when we are about to embark on self-defeating behavior.

"I feel there are two people inside me—me and my intuition. If I go against her, she'll screw me every time, and if I follow her, we get along quite nicely."

—Kim Basinger

Inner Bitch 101

An Inner Bitch Reminder:

Judy Garland once said: "Be a first rate version of yourself, not a second rate version of someone else."
Dare to be an original today!

Our Inner Bitch makes us willing to speak our minds. We may not always be right, but being right isn't always the point. Speaking our minds is.

What the Inner Bitch is not is destructive. She is not stupid, or mean, or humorless, or abusive to Herself or others. Oh, and she doesn't hate men or blame them for...well, anything.

The Inner Bitch does not engage in petty arguments, even for sport. Why bother? Though She is perfectly capable of a witty comeback along the lines of "I'll try being nicer if you'll try being smarter." Your Inner Bitch always fights fair—she knows the difference between stating her position and going for the jugular.

The Inner Bitch never enters into a battle of wits with an unarmed opponent. And she is never afraid to say, "Screw 'em if they can't take a joke."

I hold this truth to be self-evident: By getting in touch with our Inner Bitch, we are free to tap into Her power and energy for our own higher purposes.

If we ignore Her, we risk having her run amok when the pressure of being Nice grows too strong. We've all seen it happen; it's not a pretty sight.

When we don't acknowledge our Inner Bitch, we get pimples. Or we get fat. Or too thin, controlling, manipulative, whiny, weepy, or hysterical. We don't insist on practicing safe sex.

None of this is productive. Some of it is downright dangerous.

How do we put an end to these self-defeating behaviors, particularly after a lifetime of Toxic Niceness?

All it takes is one short phrase:

"I DON'T THINK SO."

We all think it. But we bat it away like a pesky little gnat. "That's not nice," we think. But, oh, the price we pay.

You may be asking yourself, "But can I be nice without being toxic?"

Certainly you can! In fact, being in touch with your Inner Bitch actually helps you to be truly nice. There is a world of difference between being nice and being Nice.

Your Inner Bitch does not want you to be mean. She wants you to be firm. She wants you to be reasonable. And She wants you to be kind—particularly to yourself.

The next time you feel yourself tumbling back into Toxic Niceness take heart by remembering how long it took you to really get the multiplication tables—hours of drilling them over and over, right? Apply that same approach to "I don't think so."

"The first step to getting the things you want out of life is this: decide what you want."

—Ben Stein

"There are always new, grander challenges to confront, and a true winner will embrace each one."

—Mia Hamm

Getting to "I Don't Think So"

Pick your battles. You don't have to deal with every little irritant that comes your way during the day, but never choose silence when an issue really matters or silence will lead you down the path to Toxic Niceness.

Give it a shot. Start out with small increments. Think of a situation in your life where it might be applicable. For example:

�֍ Your 22-year-old daughter wants to move into her old bedroom, rent-free, with her lover and his motorcycle.

　　You say: "I don't think so."

�֍ The man you've been dating for a month demands in a fit of jealousy that you cancel a dinner meeting with an important client.

　　Your response: "I don't think so."

✷ Your mother wants you to meet the son of her bridge partner. "Just a little dinner, darling. We've made reservations for you at the Four Seasons after the theater."

　　You smile: "Mom, I don't think so."

✳ Your boss strongly suggests that you invest your year-end bonus in his cousin's latest venture.

　　You: "I don't think so."

Saying Less, Meaning More

"Being a sex symbol has to do with attitude, not looks. Most men think it's looks, most women know otherwise."

—Kathleen Turner

"I don't think so" has come under some heavy criticism from pundits and malcontents. They believe that the phrase is wimpy, annoying, and ultimately ineffective because it's perceived as "nagging."

I don't think so. Critics of the phrase "I don't think so" claim it's annoying—but your Inner Bitch knows they say that because they hear it so often. Think about that.

Look at the power in those four simple words! No one can mistake their meaning and arguing against the phrase is futile—how can anyone claim that you do think so if you say you don't think so? Particularly in the earliest stages of getting in touch, being able to respond to obnoxious requests and suggestions with "I don't think so" is incredibly empowering.

It's gentle. It's polite. At the same time, it's strong, firm, and indisputable. The more we use our muscles, the stronger they get. The same thing works with our Inner Bitch. Flex your "I don't think so" muscles frequently.

Your Inner Bitch wants to remind you that Toxic Niceness "shoulds" all over you. When that little voice inside your head starts up, just say "I don't think so"—unless it's saying something like, "You really should get outside and enjoy the weekend. After all, summer only lasts three months."

An Inner Bitch Reminder:

Just because you said yes to something the first time doesn't mean you have to keep on doing it.

The best thing about "I don't think so" is that it can be used at any time during a conversation. If you catch yourself sliding into Toxic Niceness, it's very easy to break the fall. And if you forget to say it, don't worry—

the opportunity is guaranteed to come up again. The next time you need to set a boundary with someone (which ought to happen any second now), remember that "I don't think so" can buy you time to think.

"Great works are performed, not by strength, but by perseverance."

—Samuel Johnson

Saying More

Practice saying "I don't think so" in the shower, while you're driving, when you're putting on your makeup, whenever. The more you say it, the more naturally it will roll off your tongue.

Naturally, there are times when "I don't think so" isn't enough. It's a base upon which to build, to make a sort of verbal sundae. Heap on as many toppings as you like.

When a friend calls you at work—for the fifth time today—asking if you have time to talk: "I don't think so. Unless, of course, you promise to support me after I get the boot."

✳ ✳ ✳

When the head of the bake sale committee asks you the night before the sale to make a few dozen more of "your wonderful hand decorated cupcakes because they always sell so well"—"I don't think so, but I'll gladly show you how to make them before the next event."

✳ ✳ ✳

When a friend asks to borrow your great-grandmother's diamond earrings because they'll look great with her new outfit—"I don't think so, but you're welcome to the cubic zirconia copies I had made."

✳ ✳ ✳

When the pushy saleswoman urges you to actually buy the outrageous print ensemble that just happens to match the outfit she's wearing—"I don't think that's a good color for me." You know it's multicolored, she's knows it's multicolored, and your point will be made.

✳ ✳ ✳

When the guy you've dated twice wants you to invite him in at the end of the night—"I don't think I'm ready for that."

Then there are those cases that require a certain delicacy combined with an ability to think on your feet:

You are at a party talking with ten of your closest personal acquaintances. A friend of a friend introduces himself to you and says, "Do you know Jim told me you're the perfect woman for me?" At this point, you might say,

"I don't think so, but hum a few bars."

You see, the phrase is polite and reasonable, never cruel, and not hard to say. Try different tones of voice. Give it a musing tone, or try putting the emphasis on different words: I don't think so. I don't think so.

I THINK I'D LIKE
TO BE LESS OF A
SWEETiE PiE
AND MORE
OF A
BiTCH.

"You only start being called bitch when you become successful."

⌒

—Judith Regan

T P.R. Problem

f us may have a problem claiming the term
for ourselves. We may believe that to do
ffirm the negative image assertive women
for years. To wit: if we say what we really
e must be a bitch. Your Inner Bitch wants you
nsider this: when we speak our minds, we're
ong women. When "those other women" do the
same thing, they're just being nasty bitches. Let's stop
that right now.

This question could keep sociologists and theorists
busy for years, perhaps decades. That's fine. They need
some way to justify the grant money. The simple truth
is this: the true cause of the P.R. problem for the Inner
Bitch is fear of being called a bitch.

After all, bitch is also a word that's synonymous with
complaining, usually about something inconsequential
or petty—like equal rights or being treated with respect

According to Webster's Third I
International Dictionary, "bitc
is a generalized term of abuse,
"Bitch goddess," on the other han
is defined as
"a material or worldly success."
Your Inner Bitch wants to you think
about this.

or having the same opportunities as men. "Bitch, bitch, bitch," is usually a retort akin to "waah, waah, waah," and the desirable result is that whoever is doing the complaining will quit their whining. Your Inner Bitch wants you to consider this: if we say what we really think, we must be a bitch. Why is that? Are we really behaving badly? Or are we just going too fast, getting too far ahead, breaking out of our designated niche? Why is it that we're usually called "bitch" when we're right?

> "Life's a bitch and then they call you one."
>
> —Mary Frances Connelly

This is becoming less of an issue, of course. Entire media empires are dedicated to promoting assertive self-expression and letting go of Toxic Niceness and its many pseudonyms. Women are increasingly proud of feeling a little bit like outlaws and are actually being rewarded for making bold moves. "Bitch" has, increasingly, become a word that conveys a certain level of respect and affection when referring to strong, outspoken women.

An Inner Bitch Reminder: "Bitch" also rhymes with "Rich."

But that word. That word is just so...oh, I don't know, direct? In your face? And I get that to a degree. After all, I've experienced being called a bitch in the negative sense of the word for...well, let's just say a long time.

"Nobody objects to a woman being a good writer or sculptor or geneticist if at the same time she manages to be a good wife, good mother, good-looking, good-tempered, well-groomed and unaggressive."

—Leslie McIntyre

In other words, nobody objects to a woman being good at her profession as long as she's Nice, as long as she's not a bitch. Hmmm. Can you say "double bind?" Sure you can.

What exactly is the problem here? When we get labeled "bitch" are we really behaving badly? Or are we just going too fast, getting too far ahead, and breaking out of our designated niche?

Chapter Three
The P.R. Problem

Some of us may have a problem claiming the term "bitch" for ourselves. We may believe that to do so would affirm the negative image assertive women have borne for years. To wit: if we say what we really think, we must be a bitch. Your Inner Bitch wants you to consider this: when we speak our minds, we're strong women. When "those other women" do the same thing, they're just being nasty bitches. Let's stop that right now.

This question could keep sociologists and theorists busy for years, perhaps decades. That's fine. They need some way to justify the grant money. The simple truth is this: the true cause of the P.R. problem for the Inner Bitch is fear of being called a bitch.

After all, bitch is also a word that's synonymous with complaining, usually about something inconsequential or petty—like equal rights or being treated with respect

According to Webster's Third New International Dictionary, "bitch" is a generalized term of abuse. "Bitch goddess," on the other hand, is defined as "a material or worldly success." Your Inner Bitch wants to you think about this.

An Inner Bitch Reminder: "Bitch" also rhymes with "Rich."

But that word. That word is just so...oh, I don't know, direct? In your face? And I get that to a degree. After all, I've experienced being called a bitch in the negative sense of the word for...well, let's just say a long time.

"Nobody objects to a woman being a good writer or sculptor or geneticist if at the same time she manages to be a good wife, good mother, good-looking, good-tempered, well-groomed and unaggressive."

—Leslie McIntyre

In other words, nobody objects to a woman being good at her profession as long as she's Nice, as long as she's not a bitch. Hmmm. Can you say "double bind?" Sure you can.

What exactly is the problem here? When we get labeled "bitch" are we really behaving badly? Or are we just going too fast, getting too far ahead, and breaking out of our designated niche?

or having the same opportunities as men. "Bitch, bitch, bitch," is usually a retort akin to "waah, waah, waah," and the desirable result is that whoever is doing the complaining will quit their whining. Your Inner Bitch wants you to consider this: if we say what we really think, we must be a bitch. Why is that? Are we really behaving badly? Or are we just going too fast, getting too far ahead, breaking out of our designated niche? Why is it that we're usually called "bitch" when we're right?

"Life's a bitch and then they call you one."

—Mary Frances Connelly

This is becoming less of an issue, of course. Entire media empires are dedicated to promoting assertive self-expression and letting go of Toxic Niceness and its many pseudonyms. Women are increasingly proud of feeling a little bit like outlaws and are actually being rewarded for making bold moves. "Bitch" has, increasingly, become a word that conveys a certain level of respect and affection when referring to strong, outspoken women.

"Bitch" has much more history as a weapon against uppity women than as a term of wry affection and recognition. Calling us bitches puts us on notice that it is time to beat a hasty retreat to Toxic Niceness.

All I can say is, "I don't think so."

Consider this point: Just as most women have been trained in the ways of Toxic Niceness, men have been trained in the ways of whatever it is they're suffering from—some of which is probably counter to their true nature. So cut them a break, but don't spend too much time analyzing them. And don't let them off the hook. The phrase "boys will be boys" seems to equal a lifetime of freedom from Toxic Niceness. Let's start giving girls permission to be girls.

Can a man be in touch with his Inner Bitch? Does he even have an Inner Bitch? Of course. But is he sporting this book? I don't think so.

> *"We're our own worst enemy a lot of the time, but I still blame men."*
>
> —Janeane Garofalo

While it's tempting to point fingers and blame only men for using the word "bitch" against us, that's just not true. Women use the word "bitch" as a weapon—usually against women who are more successful than we are, more forthright than we are, more comfortable with a sense of entitlement than we are...even more attractive than we are. We can even hold grudges against these women beyond their actual presence in our life.

For instance, a self-acknowledged fan of the Inner Bitch once gleefully recounted the life history of her high school nemesis. "Oh, she was such a bitch! She was the captain of the cheerleaders, and she was just so cute and perky, and now she's a hairdresser," this woman crowed, as if hairdressers weren't among the most powerful people in the world. (Admit it; we live in fear of the dreaded "bad haircut.") More to the point, as if being perky, cute, and captain of the cheerleaders—all incredibly powerful things in your average high school—was a punishable offense that bitch had nearly gotten away with.

A dirty little secret is that Toxic Niceness works best when women are set apart from one another. Because who knows what kind of earth-shattering changes might happen if women actually supported one another? The bitches might take over the whole world!

"When I was eighteen, nineteen, twenty, I would see a woman baking cookies, or toting around a bunch of kids, or wearing lipstick, and a tight dress, and I'd think, 'Oh, please, baby—liberate yourself.' I've come to realize...who am I to decide what women's liberation looks or smells like?"

—Ani DiFranco

While we'll admit that we have, on occasion, resorted to bitchy behavior ourselves, it's only because our hands were forced. In our more candid moments, we'll talk about our bitchiness with gleeful pride. Because, let's face it, there have been times in all our lives when being a bitch was fun. We all know it's true.

"Men make angry music and it's called rock-and-roll; women include anger in their vocabulary and suddenly they're angry and militant."

—Ani Difranco

But ask us if we consider ourselves bitches and we will say no. Oh no, no, no, no, NO! We consider ourselves Nice Girls who are occasionally backed against the wall and must defend ourselves by acting like bitches. It's one thing to indulge ourselves in a little prickly behavior now and then. It's even okay to celebrate our strength and power. It's quite another to accept a vision of ourselves as strong, powerful and—egads!—demanding women who expect more from life's banquet than a few little crumbs and are willing to put their expectations out there for the whole world to see. It's those "other women" who really are bitches. You know who they are.

Again, I don't think so.

In fact, I think that this dynamic carries in it the seeds of divisiveness. A dirty little secret is that Toxic Niceness works best when we are set apart from one another, when we are divided and disrespect each other. Because who knows what kind of earth-shattering changes might happen if women actually supported one another?

"I am not an eccentric. It's just that I am more alive than most people. I am an unpopular electric eel in a pool of catfish."

—Edith Sitwell

The bitches might take over the whole world.

If I've Got the Name, I Want the Game

Any woman who succeeds at anything is going to be called a bitch. Madonna? Bitch. Hillary Clinton? Bitch. Martha Stewart? Bitch. Barbra Streisand? Bitch. The list goes on and on and on and...

You know, if no one has called you a bitch lately, you're probably on the slippery slope toward Toxic Niceness.

The point is that since we can't avoid it, why don't we embrace it? We've all had this experience: At some point in time, in front of other people, we say what we really think about some issue or person or what-have-you. At some later point in time, someone tells us that, "So-and-so really thought you were a bitch." (If it hasn't happened yet, just keep talking—it will.)

Remember these two things:

- Any woman who speaks her mind, is out to change the world, or shows her full intelligence and power is apt to be called a bitch.
- Any successful woman is going to be called a bitch.

Since we can't avoid it, let's wear the title as a badge of honor!

Most of us make sure to be particularly nice to old so-and-so next time we see them. We may even go out of our way to prove that perceiving us as a bitch is not only erroneous, but downright unfair. Or we explain away all the reasons we said whatever it was we said. "I was under a lot of stress last time we met," or, "Gosh, I don't know what came over me!" Or even, "It must have been the hormones."

We retreat.

What if we responded by sending so-and-so a thank-you bouquet with a little card that said, "I really appreciate your recognition of my Inner Bitch."

What would happen if we stopped being afraid of this one little word?

"Women complain about premenstrual syndrome, but I think of it as the only time of the month that I can be myself."

—Roseanne Barr

Your Inner Bitch would like to remind you that, just because you may actually be experiencing PMS doesn't mean that you're not completely justified in bitching about some absurd situation.

Another point that must be made, which requires a short foray into rhetoric: What do we call a man who speaks up for himself, a man who is demanding of himself and those around him, a man who behaves as any self-respecting bitch would? A success.

"Why is it that men must be bastards and women must wear pearls and smile?"

—Lynn Hecht Schafren

Who Is to Blame For This?

Well, no one. Maybe everyone. One point about the Inner Bitch is so important, however, that it must be stated in no uncertain terms:

THE INNER BITCH IS NOT ABOUT BLAME.

The Inner Bitch simply is, just as the sky is simply the sky, and dishes, once dirty, must be washed. There is no need to point a finger at anyone. Nor is there a reason to apologize for being in touch with Her. After all, She is the part of us that knows what we really care about and want.

She knows that we take pride in our work and that we hold ourselves and others to a certain standard.

She knows that we want our lovers to please us sexually (more about this later).

She knows that we want our friend, the Bride, to understand that wearing taffeta after the age of twelve is embarrassing. The Inner Bitch wants our friend, the Bride, to understand that we all know the real reason behind those bridesmaids' dresses. And we love her anyway.

She knows that we want the world to take the measure of our accomplishments, not of our bodies. She knows that we want to be able to say what we know, without being called names.

As long as we deny that the Inner Bitch is part of us, as long as we succumb to Toxic Niceness, we will not get what we want. We will not get what we need. And none of us will really get what is good for all of us.

"Let the world know you as you are, not as you think you should be, because sooner or later, if you are posing, you will forget the pose, and then where are you?"

—Fanny Brice

"Real sisterhood [is]...a bunch of dames in bathrobes throwing back M&Ms and making each other laugh."

—Maxine Wilkie

Chapter Four
Can We Talk!

*I*t doesn't really get any better than this: a bunch of women gathered together with time to talk. And what do we women do when we talk? We get to the bottom of things. It's beautiful. You've got to have friends. So why not make sure that those friends are in touch with their Inner Bitch and honor yours? Our friends who are in touch with their Inner Bitches are the ones we can count on to keep us in touch with our dreams, our aspirations, and our best selves.

Your Inner Bitch wants you to consider what one wise woman once said: "Friends are like bras: close to your heart and there for support."

The Inner Bitch
as a Teenager

We start in adolescence, when we struggle with everything. That's when we discover how insightful our friends are, how well they understand everything.

They sympathize with us about the unreasonable curfew, and the impossible history exam; they commiserate with us over the painful braces, the boy who doesn't call, and the new shirt that shrinks in the wash; and they swoon with us over our teen idols.

Once we have recovered from our teens (and most of us do, eventually), we are able to form strong, valuable friendships with other women. Our best friendships are ones in which we meet each other head-on with our Inner Bitch. The best thing about close friends is that they know the whole story—every little detail. That is a treasure beyond measure, especially if they are in touch with their Inner Bitch.

As my friends and I struggle with our tendencies toward Toxic Niceness, our Inner Bitch compels us to set boundaries that keep our friendships healthy. Emotional blackmail? Betraying secrets? Nasty gossip?

I don't think so.

Friends Indeed

"Female friendships that work are relationships in which women help each other belong to themselves."

—Louise Bernikow

It isn't always easy for women who are in touch with their Inner Bitches to be friends, because the rules that govern relationships between women are so complex that the Gordian knot looks like a child's puzzle in comparison. But these friendships are so much more meaningful than those relationships that are based on Toxic Niceness.

They say, "It's lonely at the top." The Inner Bitch says, "Bring your friends along." How else are we going to break up the old boy's club?

Our friends who are in touch with their Inner Bitch are often the most supportive, the ones to whom we turn when we feel our resolve begin to slip in the face of unreasonable bosses and impossible deadlines, the lover who suddenly stops calling, the expensive earring lost. They are the ones who remind us of the importance of our dreams and aspirations, quietly or loudly urging us forward when the path seems too steep or long.

> *"I can trust my friends. These people force me to examine myself, encourage me to grow."*
>
> —Cher

The primary element of women's bonding is love. If we didn't love one another, we wouldn't bother telling the truth. We'd just let one another lurch from one delusion to the next, gathering up enough experience to make blues singers of all of us.

> *"Friendship with oneself is all important because without it one cannot be friends with anybody else in the world."*
>
> —Eleanor Roosevelt

The beauty of getting in touch with our Inner Bitch is that we can then hear our own voices. The Inner Bitch knows what She knows. And She's not afraid to say it. But it is up to us to listen. The fact is, after we have had enough experience with jive, we can see it coming. And we can sometimes pull a good friend out of harm's way.

> "It's the ones you can call up at 4:00 a.m. that matter."
>
> —Marlene Dietrich

For example, when our friend's Joe breaks her heart by running off to help his buddy start a business in Hawaii, do we point out that we'd told her so? Of course not. Being in touch with our Inner Bitch requires sensitivity.

She: "I can't believe he left me! And to live some-place that's warm all year, too! Maybe I should follow him."

You: "Do you know how many toxic insects there are in Hawaii?"

Then we make sure to get together often to watch movies like *Thelma and Louise* or *The Lion in Winter* and order take-out food (anything but poi). Eventually we move on to extremely romantic films set in locations like Alaska, taking care to point out how sexy it is to find out exactly what's under that parka.

The next time you're on the verge of doing something that's not in your best interest, ask yourself this: "If I were to tell my best friend about this, would she slap me silly?"

SYLVIA   by Nicole Hollander

"Love me in full being."

—Elizabeth Barrett Browning

By the same token, in the unlikely event that you find yourself trying to "break in" a boyfriend by getting him to change in some way, your Inner Bitch wants you to ask yourself if this is how you want to spend your time—or your life

"If sex and creativity are often seen by dictators as subversive activities, it's because they lead to the knowledge that you own your own body (and with it your own voice), and that's the most revolutionary insight of all."

—Erica Jong

Let's face it: Romance is where Toxic Niceness is most prevalent. And where it is most dangerous, too.

An Inner Bitch Reminder:

If a lasting relationship wasn't the goal, we'd never put up with the horrors of dating.

Because many of us are afraid that if the ones we love really knew us, they wouldn't want anything to do with us. But if they don't know the real us, we live in fear that they will no longer love us if we reveal ourselves to them. So we dedicate ourselves to being thoughtful, agreeable, helpful, sweet, and nice, nice, nice.

Unfortunately, no one can pull this off for a lifetime. Eventually Toxic Niceness is going to come to an end in the nastiest of ways.

Uttering the words, "If you really loved me..." is absolutely the last thing a woman who's in touch with her Inner Bitch would say. Of course he loves you—you wouldn't be hanging around with him if he didn't.

It might happen when, for the 10,000th time in a row, our beloved neglects to put in a new garbage bag after taking out the trash, which he always does just as we're beginning to make dinner and we really need to get rid of the chicken innards and-when-did-making-dinner-become-my-job-anyway?

It might happen while we're deciding which movie to see and we just will not subject ourselves to another action-packed extravaganza featuring an aging male star who is fated to end up with the beautiful starlet who's half his age.

It might happen when our beloved offers another "helpful" suggestion about our golf game, a situation at work, our workout or, perhaps, not actually eating the entire bag of M&Ms in one sitting (even though he knows what time of the month it is).

We've been trained to believe that intimacy somehow equals telepathy, that our "soul mate" should be able to read our minds. Hogwash. We can't even read our own minds half the time.

Whatever the precipitating event, we explode and years of being Nice are washed away in a stream of invectives, we end up in tears and, ultimately, feelings of incredible remorse toss us back into the waiting arms of Toxic Niceness. And the pressure begins to build once more.

Golly, now there's a vicious cycle! Being in touch with our Inner Bitch leads the way out of that cycle.

One thing the Inner Bitch knows for sure: Ask for what you want. Subtle hints do not work. Strong hints do not work. Obvious hints do not work. Just say it.

An Inner Bitch Reminder:

Do not think for one second that Toxic Niceness is going to get you the relationship you really want and really deserve.

An Inner Bitch reminder:

"I didn't want to hurt his feelings" is not
a sufficient reason to sleep with someone. Neither is
"I don't know, it just happened."

The Toxic Way to Intimacy

It usually starts with the first date. Here's a scenario in which Toxic Niceness is at work:

Prospective Love Partner: "I was thinking we should go see a movie."

Toxic Nice Girl: "Okay."

In reality, Toxic Nice Girl hates movies and would prefer to do something more interactive, like shoot pool. But she is unwilling to say so, for fear that her date will think she's too pushy, or too demanding, or...a bitch.

*"Women are not inherently passive or peaceful.
We're not inherently anything but human."*

—Robin Morgan

During that first date, Toxic Nice Girl will undoubtedly behave as if she is actually enjoying herself, when what she really wants is a chance to get to know this guy. She will also probably thank him for a wonderful time, all the while thinking, "If he really likes me, eventually we'll do what I want to do."

Your Inner Bitch doesn't want you to waste time chasing love down romantic cul-de-sacs. Read the "dead end" signs; you know what they look like.

Of course, they never do. Toxic Nice Girl will continue to acquiesce until she feels she's in a powerful enough position to actually demand that she get her way, usually just after her wedding. At which point her partner will be justified in wondering, "What happened to the nice girl I fell in love with?" But that's another book. Really.

"There's a study in Maine that found if you marry someone who doesn't appreciate you, tries to control you, and always has to be right, you may be unhappy. They also discovered that going without water for long periods of time makes you thirsty."

—Caroline Rhea

It is important to be in touch with our Inner Bitch before we fall in love—or into bed—with anyone.

The Inner Bitch Way to Intimacy

How much simpler it is when we are fearless from the start. Watch this:

Him: "I was thinking we should go see a movie."

Inner Bitch Girl: "I'd like to get to know you better. How about we go shoot some pool?"

This way, the guy has a good idea of what she wants right from the start. And there is room to compromise. Inner Bitch Girl has suggested doing what she wants and left the door open for a counteroffer. This starts the prospective relationship off on an equal footing.

Your Inner Bitch knows that the path to true love begins with knowing what you want—and not settling for less.

Inner Bitch Food For Thought:

Maybe our grandmothers were right when they said, "Don't worry, honey. Men are like trolleys. Miss one and another will come along soon."

Of course, the man may not want to compromise. He may, indeed, be turned off by a woman who doesn't comply with every suggestion. That sort of guy will leave eventually. But that's okay, because we don't want a Love Partner like that, do we?

I don't think so!

Five Things the Inner Bitch Knows

- Your Inner Bitch knows that a man who doesn't support your climb to the top of your profession isn't going to help you stay there.
- Your Inner Bitch knows that snooping, while nearly irresistible, is never a good idea.
- Your Inner Bitch knows that both people in a relationship are responsible for its health. She never plays Relationship Cop.
- Your Inner Bitch knows that moving in with someone as a means of "getting him to marry me" is absolutely out of the question. It is also not a dating activity—it is a relationship activity.
- Your Inner Bitch knows that the likelihood of two people sharing every interest isn't just doubtful, it's actually kind of creepy.

Sex and the Inner Bitch

Okay. Take a deep breath.

This is, admittedly, one of the most sensitive areas of our lives when it comes to the Inner Bitch. Actually, sex is one of the most sensitive issues, period. Therefore, it follows that it is most important to be in touch with our Inner Bitch before we fall into bed with anyone. Here's why.

Selectivity

"As usual, there is a great woman behind every idiot."

—John Lennon

Being in touch with our Inner Bitch ensures that we will choose carefully the people with whom we share our bodies. Your Inner Bitch knows that the phrase "He's different when we're alone" is proof that it's not your friends who are wrong.

There are loads of us who, in the interest of being nice, have ended up sleeping with people with whom we later realized we wouldn't even want to have a cup of coffee. (Come on, you know it's true!)

By the same token, in the unlikely event that you find yourself trying to "break in" a boyfriend by getting him to change in some way, your Inner Bitch wants you to ask yourself if this is how you want to spend your time—or your life

"If sex and creativity are often seen by dictators as subversive activities, it's because they lead to the knowledge that you own your own body (and with it your own voice), and that's the most revolutionary insight of all."

—Erica Jong

Let's face it: Romance is where Toxic Niceness is most prevalent. And where it is most dangerous, too.

An Inner Bitch Reminder:

If a lasting relationship wasn't the goal, we'd never put up with the horrors of dating.

Chapter Five
The Bitch in Bed

*W*ell, the Bitch in love—really. How can we maintain the Inner Bitch in that most heady arena of life, romance? If it is true that what we seek from our love partners is intimacy, then it is vital that said partners be aware of our Inner Bitch. We can't be intimate with anyone who doesn't know and respect every aspect of our personality. Real romance involves two people meeting on solid—and even—ground.

No one ever said that the Inner Bitch Way to Intimacy was going to ensure smooth sailing. But knowing what you want and being willing to tell the other person will increase the odds that you'll get what you want and need. A man who won't compromise in the beginning of a relationship won't "come around in time."

It is important to be in touch with our Inner Bitch before we fall in love—or into bed—with anyone.

The Inner Bitch Way to Intimacy

How much simpler it is when we are fearless from the start. Watch this:

Him: "I was thinking we should go see a movie."

Inner Bitch Girl: "I'd like to get to know you better. How about we go shoot some pool?"

This way, the guy has a good idea of what she wants right from the start. And there is room to compromise. Inner Bitch Girl has suggested doing what she wants and left the door open for a counteroffer. This starts the prospective relationship off on an equal footing.

Your Inner Bitch knows that the path to true love begins with knowing what you want—and not settling for less.

Inner Bitch Food For Thought:

Maybe our grandmothers were right when they said, "Don't worry, honey. Men are like trolleys. Miss one and another will come along soon."

How can we maintain the Inner Bitch
in that most heady arena of life: romance? Just keep
in touch, baby, keep in touch...

The justifications? "I didn't want to hurt his feelings."
Or, "I don't know, it just happened."

No need to beat ourselves up over having done these
things. But is it necessary to continue to do this?

I don't think so.

Orgasms

*"You get better sex when you know your own body.
How can you expect a man to know your body
when you don't know what pleases you?"*

—Eva Longoria

Toxic Niceness can be a serious impediment to sexual
satisfaction. "I didn't want him to think I was unhappy,"
Toxic Nice Girl says, after months (or years) of unsatis-
factory sex. Being in touch with our Inner Bitch ensures
that we will have orgasms. Even with other people.

And we're not afraid to have them tell us what they want, either. Everyone wins when the Bitch is in bed.

An Inner Bitch Reminder:

Don't fake orgasms. It's a completely ill-spent use of your energy, particularly if you ever want to have a real one.

Safe Sex

Being in touch with our Inner Bitch ensures that, having chosen carefully, we will not talk ourselves into believing that, by virtue of niceness, it would be impossible for our partner (or us) to have a sexually transmitted disease. Niceness does not immunize anyone.

Insisting on practicing safe sex may be difficult, but consider the alternatives. So, how does the Inner Bitch broach the subject? Forthrightly, that's how.

Like this, for example:

Everything is just right, the lights are low, music is playing softly, and you've spent the entire evening testing the waters, so to speak. You come up for air, gaze into each other's eyes. Neither of you want to break the spell of the moment, but you know you must.

"Sweetheart," you say. "Are there condoms in the house?"

"No, my love," he replies. "But you can trust me."

"I don't think so," you say, pulling yourself together.

If his response is, "No, but I'll run down to the all-night drugstore," by all means, offer to drive.

And remember, we are adults now. It's okay for us to carry condoms.

Relationships and intimacy require hard work—and your Inner Bitch is nothing if not a hard worker.

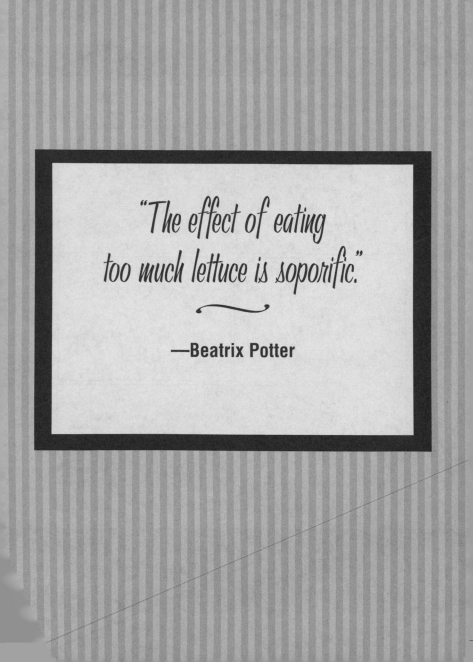

"The effect of eating too much lettuce is soporific."

—Beatrix Potter

Chapter Six
Glorious Food

Q: "What does the Inner Bitch make for dinner?"

A: "A choice."

The Inner Bitch is a powerful ally to have in the ongoing struggle between our minds and our bodies. For example, my mind says, "Grains, veggies, fruit." My body tends to say, "Melted cheese, melted cheese, chocolate." What role does my Inner Bitch play in all this? Voice of reason, voice of stomach.

"The first thing I did when I made the decision to kill myself was to stop dieting. Let them dig a wider hole."

—Gail Parent

That's right; food is the one area where even the Inner Bitch plays both sides: one day it's "grains, veggies, fruit," the next it can be "melted cheese, melted cheese, melted chocolate."

Your Inner Bitch knows that resisting temptation is often a good choice. So is giving in to it. Choose wisely.

"If you have enough butter, anything is good."

—Julia Child

The difference is that being in touch with my Inner Bitch keeps the whole thing in perspective. She allows me to honor my food cravings while remembering to maintain good health. However, your Inner Bitch understands that seasonal foods are best. That's why it's important to eat plenty of fresh peach ice cream during peach season.

"Veni, Vidi, Vegi...I came, I saw, I had a salad."

—Anonymous (and we know she's a woman)

Does this phrase sound familiar? "Oh, I've been really bad!"

Of course it does, and it's not sex we're talking about. No, we are almost always referring to something that we've eaten. Chocolate, perhaps; French fries; fettuccine Alfredo; if we consume anything beyond lettuce and a Diet Coke, we judge ourselves with the harshness of Calvinists. And usually condemn ourselves to several days of eating nothing but bottled spring water and the odd carrot or celery stick. This we refer to as "being good."

But the question must be posed: Is it good to be cranky and light-headed?

I don't think so!

Your Inner Bitch would like to suggest removing the phrase "I've been really bad" from your diet. Those potato chips were just one choice; you can make another one later today. Or tomorrow.

*"Nobody's last words have been
'I wish I'd eaten more rice cakes.'"*

—Amy Krouse Rosenthal

How can we think and act in our best interest when we're obsessed with calorie counts, bathroom scales, and tape measures?

Here's some happy news: research has proven that chocolate is good for you. Take that in. Good. For. You. Sharing is also good.

"If we're not willing to settle for junk living, we certainly shouldn't settle for junk food."

—Sally Edwards

Your Inner Bitch knows that haste makes waist—let's just say no to fat-saturated, carb-loaded, truly unhealthy fast food.

Inside me lives a skinny
woman crying to get out.
But I can usually shut her
up with chocolate!

Back to Basics

"When I'm hungry, I eat. When I'm thirsty, I drink. When I feel like saying something, I say it."

—Madonna

Our Inner Bitch reminds us that food is basic to survival, not to mention peace of mind. Sometimes, food is just plain comforting. What could be better after a really wretched day than a big bowl of garlic mashed potatoes? Or an entire bag of peanut M&Ms—the one-pounder, not the single serving size? It may be that our Inner Bitch could have prevented us from having a wretched day in the first place, but once it's happened, our Inner Bitch knows that any means of saving a day from being a total wipeout is a good thing.

"God made a very obvious choice when he made me voluptuous; why would I go against what He decided for me? My limbs work, so I'm not going to complain about the way my body is shaped."

—Drew Barrymore

Your Inner Bitch wants you to consider the wise words of Peter de Vries: "Gluttony is an emotional escape, a sign something is eating us." In other words, don't substitute eating a piece of cake for giving someone a piece of your mind. Have you ever realized suddenly that you just ate an entire bag of chips, but you don't remember doing it? Your Inner Bitch wants you to stop doing stuff like that—eat chips, or whatever, consciously so you can enjoy the experience.

"Food is like sex: when you abstain, even the worst stuff begins to look good."

—Beth McCollister

The bottom line: Eat what you want, whether it's strawberries or ice cream or pulled pork barbecue. And remember that there will be another opportunity to enjoy these things, so you can say no (or the trusty "I don't think so") to that third helping.

The Bitchin' Kitchen

Food can also be an event, an opportunity to make contact with the important people in our lives.

Some of us find the process of getting and preparing food calming and creative. Some of us go to great lengths to avoid everything but its consumption. It doesn't really matter where you are on the spectrum, because the mechanics of food aren't the issue. What is the issue is that food must be dealt with. And our Inner Bitch allows us to make food arrangements that work for us.

When we are in touch with our Inner Bitch, we don't have to create a ten-course meal for in-laws who have never been kind to us, or for business associates who don't support us, or for friends with a tin palate.

Perhaps the most important point is this: Our Inner Bitch takes food, and all the rituals surrounding food, seriously. But She is not taken in by the tyrannies of fashion.

Your Inner Bitch knows that, while they are handy, calling those microwavable dinners a "meal" doesn't make it so.

What does our Inner Bitch have to say about diets that require a grown woman to consume fewer calories than a two-year-old?

"I don't think so."

> *"I really don't think I need buns of steel.*
> *I'd be happy with buns of cinnamon."*
>
> —Ellen DeGeneres

What is Her response to the expectation that all women—no matter what their natural body type—should wear clothing no larger than size twelve?

"I don't think so."

Our Inner Bitch sees the absurdity of trying to look like someone else, when each of us is already such a beauty.

*"Oh, honey, I would...
but I don't want to."*

—Karen Walker, *Will and Grace*

Chapter Seven
Daily Life

*W*e may think of our Inner Bitch only in connection with special occasions, sort of like a party dress or lipstick. Our thoughts might go something like this: "I'll just save my Inner Bitch for when I really need Her. After all, I wouldn't want to wear Her out." As if the Inner Bitch were a pair of cheap shoes with flimsy soles. Could something this powerful be so fragile?

I don't think so.

"The biggest sin is sitting on your ass."

—Florynce R. Kennedy

The Inner Bitch is a vital part of our daily lives.

It is necessary, however, to practice discernment when utilizing Her power.

The Leisurely Inner Bitch

If you're wondering whether it's a good day to be in touch with your Inner Bitch, remember this: she is the little black dress of attitudes, perfect for every occasion.

Your Inner Bitch knows you're probably exhausted, so she wants you to take a break—fix yourself a nice bubble bath, get take-out tonight, or simply sit down for ten minutes. Limit the demands you and others place on your time and energy and dedicate yourself to one thing—preferably getting a massage or something. Your Inner Bitch wants you to make time for pampering—however you define it. Oh, and just to be clear, She means pampering yourself.

**Remember the first Inner Bitch rule
of fighting fair:**

**Know what you're really angry about.
It's probably not that the other
person took the last slice of pizza.**

Can't we all just agree that the occasional day devoted completely to pleasure—whether it's eating chocolate or taking a good long hike (or shopping trip) with our best friend—is life-affirming?

Knowing the Difference

There are always going to be things about which we can do nothing—traffic, lines at the grocery store, increased activity on the surface of the Sun. Do we rant and rave at these things?

I don't think so.

We can take some comfort from the knowledge that we have no power over some situations—the Inner Bitch doesn't bother expending energy on things that are beyond Her control.

"Being told to sit still and enjoy myself is logically incompatible."

—Leslie Glendower Peabody

At the same time, it would take a saint not to react to the pressure caused by those things that are out of our control. And maybe not reacting is a sign of Toxic Niceness. Be that as it may, the important thing to remember is that the Inner Bitch can help us to respond, rather than react, to situations that are out of our control.

Making "I Don't Think So" Work for Us

Your Inner Bitch wants you to remember Ambrose Bierce's definition of politeness: "The most acceptable hypocrisy." Keep that in mind the next time you have to write a thank you note for a truly hideous present.

Take a typical day. We step out every morning to conduct our lives and something happens. Something always happens. We are waiting on line at the deli for our bagel (lightly toasted, with just a bit of cream cheese), and when the person behind the counter asks who is next, someone steps in front of us, saying, "I am," and begins ordering from a list—typed single-spaced on a sheet of legal paper.

We go shopping at the mall. As we enter the upscale anchor department store, we encounter the ubiquitous purveyor of perfumes standing at the ready with her atomizer and well-rehearsed spiel about how this scent will change our lives. "Would you care to experience Raison d'être?" she asks. Your Inner Bitch knows that those people in department stores who spray cologne at us with no provocation are simply trying to make a living. So she suggests fending them off with a preemptive "I don't think so" rather than, say, a running tackle.

Perhaps we encounter another driver in a parking lot. The type of encounter in which that driver backs into our passenger side. The impact of the collision dislodges the sideview mirror, an inconvenience that (according to the other driver) will have little impact on our lives. "The rearview mirror's all ya really need anyway, sweetie," he says.

> *"Is your remarkably sexist drivel intentional, or just some horrible mistake?"*
>
> —Lisa Simpson

"Sooner or later we all discover that the important moments in life are not the advertised ones, not the birthdays, the graduations, the weddings, not the great goals achieved. The real milestones are less prepossessing. Our lives are measured by these."

—Susan B. Anthony

To each of these situations we can respond, "I don't think so."

This takes some practice. At first, the prospect of a direct confrontation may fill us with dread. But practice does indeed make for proficiency. And most people respond rather well to hearing the Inner Bitch mantra spoken aloud. The next time you're stuck in traffic or a long line, pass the time by making a mental list of all the movie and TV characters that are in touch with their Inner Bitch. By the time you've reached your destination you're sure to be feeling more powerful.

"Excuse me," we say to the line cutter. "I don't think so. I believe I was here first."

"Raison d'être? I don't think so." It may be necessary to shield ourselves in some way from the shower of perfume that inevitably follows fast on the heels of the offer.

"I don't think so. I want your insurance information," we say to our new buddy.

What can they say in response, really? Is anyone going to argue?

Well, certainly there is a percentage of the population that will argue. There are plenty of people who hurl themselves into a perfectly absurd defense of just the sort of indefensible behavior referred to here.

Do we shrink in the face of this phenomenon?

I don't think so.

The mantra of the Inner Bitch is especially helpful when we are presented with unreasonable estimates for minor car repairs, when we are asked to "please hold" for the umpteenth time, and when others attempt to bully us into doing things for them.

Indeed, the phrase, "I don't think so," becomes more powerful the more we say it.

SYLVIA

by Nicole Hollander

the Woman who Worries about Everything drops the Ball and Look what almost Happened.

I'M NOT PERFECT.

4-29

I GOT VERY BUSY

AND I FORGOT RUSSIA.

HONEY, I'M GLAD YOU'RE BACK ON the JOB.

"The Inner Bitch knows it's a cliché, but it bears repeating: "A woman's place is in the House, the Senate, and the Oval Office."

—**Anonymous**

Chapter Eight
Personal Politics

*T*he major concern of our Inner Bitch is, naturally, our life. Just getting through the day takes so much energy that there's very little left over for anything else. Laundry? It has to get done, so we do it. Sleep? We'd die without it. Work? Well, our survival often depends on our ability to provide for ourselves. It's entirely understandable that most of us don't have much time to devote to politics. Besides, what does it really matter?

"If you have any doubts that we live in a society controlled by men, try reading down the index of contributors to a volume of quotations, looking for women's names."

—Elaine Gill

Well, let's take a look at this, shall we?

Part of the Problem

It's entirely understandable that most of us don't have time for politics, but consider this: if we continue to enter politics at the rate we have been, it will be three hundred years before there's an equal number of women and men in the U.S. Congress. Do we have time to wait? I don't think so.

Your Inner Bitch doesn't tolerate injustices, because she knows that's Toxic Niceness in the making.

Who's going to write laws that are good for women? We already know the answer. In light of that answer, we really must do more.

"More?" you say.

Yes, I say. I'm not talking about taking on another activity, or running for Congress (or even the school board), or doing something that will tip us over into the exhaustion that threatens every one of us. I'm talking about using our Inner Bitch to make a better world.

> *"If women are so 'manipulative', how come more of them aren't in politics?"*
>
> —Adele Lang and Susie Rajah

You know, if there's a candidate out there who's worth supporting or a cause worth taking up, your Inner Bitch wants you to do so.

"I will feel equality has arrived when we can elect to office women who are as incompetent as some of the men who are already there."

—Maureen Reagan

The Inner Bitch wonders when we'll get a long weekend in celebration of an extraordinary woman?

An Inner Bitch Statistic:

Women control 51.3 percent of the private wealth in the United States. Just thought you should know.

An Inner Bitch History Lesson:

On December 1, 1955, Rosa Parks was arrested for refusing to give up her seat on the bus, sparking the Montgomery bus boycott.
Who says simple actions can't change the world?

Part of the Solution

The easiest thing to do is to vote with our dollars. That's right, don't buy those products whose advertising belittles women, insults us, or raises by another notch or two the already unrealistic standards to which we hold ourselves. This takes thought and awareness, and not much time.

"In politics if you want anything said, ask a man. If you want anything done, ask a woman."

—Margaret Thatcher

If the stores we shop in don't carry products that please us, it's up to us to let them know that, until our needs are met, we'll shop elsewhere. Your Inner Bitch wonders when clothing designers will realize that women want to look great and feel comfortable at the same time—and we're willing to pay good money for the pleasure. Go ahead and throw away that too-tight pair of pants or shoes.

Your Inner Bitch would like to suggest that you take some time this weekend to cruise the Internet in search of information about the amazing things women have done. Because you never know when Toxic Niceness might be about to make a comeback, and a little inspiration is a powerful antidote.

Your Inner Bitch wonders why advertising professionals still believe that the best way to sell a product to women is by making them feel inadequate. She also wonders why we're not just saying "I don't think so" and taking our money somewhere else? Think about this if you're hitting the sales today.

An Inner Bitch History Lesson:

"Sex and race, because they are easy visible differences, have been the primary ways of organizing human beings into superior and inferior groups, and into the cheap labor on which this system still depends."

—Gloria Steinem

We can turn off the radio when the offensive disk jockey starts talking.

When there's a candidate worth supporting, we can actually go to one of those fund-raising cocktail parties and we can bring friends.

"There have been women in the past far more daring than we would need to be now, who ventured all and gained a little, but survived after all."

—Germaine Greer

The next time some elected official who does not serve our needs (we know who they are) sends us a letter asking for money to run again, we can return the letter in the handy pre-addressed envelope with a note saying, "I don't think so. Not until I see some results from you. For now, I'm donating my money to Emily's List instead."

The Inner Bitch Guide to Retirement Planning

"If you don't risk anything, you risk even more."

—Erica Jong

Your Inner Bitch knows that if something sounds too good to be true, it probably isn't true at all. Consider this the next time someone suggests that you can invest $200 in their relative's latest venture and end up a millionaire. In cases like this, a little skepticism can go a long way toward protecting your retirement fund. However, your Inner Bitch wants to remind you that planning for your retirement really is a good idea.

An Inner Bitch Reminder:

Deny it all you want, but the fact is
that you're going to get older.
Don't pretend that someone else
is going to establish retirement
funds for you.

The message will be received. Think of it as taking part in a collective "I don't think so." Imagine the possibilities.

An Inner Bitch Statistic:

The average twenty-five-year-old working woman will lose more than $523,000 to unequal pay during her working life. It's time to get outraged.

"Life is to be lived. If you have to support yourself, you had bloody well better find some way that is going to be interesting."

—**Katharine Hepburn**

Chapter Nine
Work Force

*W*ork is what we do for money. Money in this society equals power. When we suffer from Toxic Niceness, we fear power. We think it is unattractive.

"As for me, I'd like to have money...I hate almost all rich people but I think I'd be darling at it."

—Dorothy Parker

We may couch this belief in phrases like "money's just not important to me," but it's really that we fear power. Which may explain why, when asked to work more without being paid more, we just say yes.

"I don't know the key to success, but the key to failure is trying to please everybody."

—Bill Cosby

When we are in touch with our Inner Bitch, we are not afraid of power. Your Inner Bitch knows that you take pride in your work—the kind you get paid for and the kind you do out of necessity. Your Inner Bitch also knows that if you're getting paid, it better not be for seventy-seven cents on the dollar.

We welcome power.

We also welcome the responsibility that comes with power. We take pride in being good at what we do, and eagerly accept new challenges. We also welcome the money, understanding that it is a manifestation of the energy we put into our work.

Your Inner Bitch knows that the best response to someone telling you "it can't be done" is to just go ahead and do it. Remember that there's a lot of truth to the saying, "It's just business, it ain't personal." So the next time someone calls you "bitch" for insisting on excellence from yourself, your co-workers, and your direct reports, give yourself a pat on the back.

We deserve all the rewards that our abilities have won us.

"I have the same goal I've had ever since I was a girl: I want to rule the world."

—Madonna

Your Inner Bitch thinks that's so cool...

Power

Power begets more power. And power can be used to make changes. Big changes. Little changes.

We all know that, but the question is, "How do we get power?"

If it's so lonely at the top, why aren't the boys up there asking us to join them?

Well, we can be certain no one will hand it to us. Therefore, perhaps the best idea is to make like Lenin, who said, "I saw power lying in the street and I picked it up." Look around. Power is at our feet, or maybe on the desk. It may take some looking, given the state of most desks, but we can find it. We see it every day when we open our eyes to it.

Pick it up!

As Gloria Steinem so famously said,
"Power can be taken, but not given."

"I don't recognize it," you say? Here are some traits of power that you may have overlooked:

Teamwork

Power is built on teamwork—think of the Sistine Chapel. Teams are built of individuals. The stronger the individuals, the stronger the team. Toxic Niceness teaches us that being part of a team means agreeing with everything everybody else says. In truth, being part of a team requires that we honestly assess each situation that faces the team and that we speak out about problems or issues.

Practice asking yourself "What am I thinking?" before using your out-loud voice. Because your Inner Bitch knows that "I was talking when I should have been listening and "What was I thinking?" are two things you don't want to find yourself saying about a professional situation.

An Inner Bitch Reminder:

It's okay to change your mind
about something.
Just remember to alert
all relevant players.

Taking Care of Business, Inner Bitch Style:

Women business owners have three top goals—to enjoy their daily work, increase profitability, and have the freedom to put into practice their own approach to work.

Your Inner Bitch knows that your ability to get things done at work depends to a large degree on other people, so it pays to get along with those other people. Does that require Toxic Niceness? I don't think so. But remember that a little give and take goes a long way.

Imagination

Power comes from imagination. Nothing has ever been created without imagination. No problem has ever been surmounted without imagination. Our Inner Bitch not only puts us in touch with our imagination, She makes us willing to speak up about it. We may not always be right, but being right isn't really the point. Speaking up is. Our contribution may spark an idea in someone else, and that idea might lead to a solution or an invention.

It's easier to apologize than to ask
for permission. Think about that the next time
you're considering a bold maneuver.

"Act as if it were impossible to fail."

—Dorothea Brand

Our Inner Bitch not only puts us in touch with our imagination, she makes us willing to find a way to express it. The medium doesn't matter—what does matter is that you have an outlet for all that creativity. She knows that creativity isn't limited to the fine arts. It's only limited by your imagination.

Knowledge

"If at first you don't succeed, destroy all evidence that you tried."

—Susan Ohanian

Power is knowledge. And knowledge is power. Each individual has knowledge no one else has. Combining everyone's knowledge begets more knowledge, the way combining rice and beans begets more protein.

"Those who are blessed with the most talent don't necessarily outperform everyone else. It's the people with follow-through who excel."

—Mary Kay Ash

According to a study by Catalyst, a research and advisory organization, the male-held stereotype that woman are poor problem-solvers creates a "catch-22" situation—because of the stereotype, people are reluctant to follow the directions of women leaders and, with their problem-solving skills undermined, women lose interpersonal power.

**Taking Care of Business,
Inner Bitch Style:**

**When you make a mistake at work,
and you will, your Inner Bitch wants
you to remember what Rosalind
Russell once said: "Flops are a part of
life's menu and I've never been a girl
to miss out on any of the courses."**

How It Works

"The last time I tried to get into the 'normal' workforce the guy told me I had to wear high heels. I'll wear the high heels, but I'm going to need a handicapped parking space."

—Margaret Smith

Every workplace depends on people working together toward a common goal, whether it's serving food, putting out a newspaper, practicing law, or whatever. The more power each individual brings to striving for the goal, the more likely it is to be attained. The road to success is dotted with many tempting parking places. The Inner Bitch says, "Keep driving."

"Help one another, is part of the religion of sisterhood."

—Louisa May Alcott

Toxic Niceness drains us of power. It follows that it also drains power from whatever work we do. We may believe that being nice will get people to do what we want them to do. Nothing could be farther from the truth.

"Think like a queen. A queen is not afraid to fail.
Failure is another stepping-stone to greatness."

—Oprah Winfrey

Which is not to say that we need to shriek and demand and throw our weight around. No, no, no! Remember— being in touch with our Inner Bitch does not mean that we get to be abusive to anyone. It simply means that we know when to be firm, when to state our position and let it be known that we will act upon our convictions.

"I don't edit myself—I say what I feel like saying even when it's the wrong thing. Sometimes I'll beat myself up for it, but you just have to let it go because if you're not present you're going to miss something good."

—Ellen DeGeneres

Toxic Nice Girls tend to acquiesce until they feel they're in a powerful enough position to actually demand getting their way. At which point their coworkers will be justified in wondering, "What happened to the nice girl we knew?"

The next time you're asked when you can squeeze another project into your already overwhelming workload, try saying this: "How about never? Does never work for you?" Make sure you smile broadly. You'll still have to do the project, but think of how gratifying that look of shock will be.

**Taking Care of Business,
Inner Bitch Style:**

Women owners of businesses with revenues of $1 million or more were more likely than men owners to have started their companies rather than have purchased, inherited, or acquired in some other way. Now that's what your Inner Bitch calls women doing it for themselves!

Rhymes with Rich

Taking Care of Business, Inner Bitch Style:

Your Inner Bitch wants you to consider the idea that the first step to getting that promotion just might be dressing the part. Look at what the women who have risen in your organization wear and put together a power wardrobe.

If it's true that you only start being called a bitch when you're successful, then we should embrace the opportunity to be called a bitch in the workplace.

Being called a bitch usually means that we are right or that we are insisting on excellence from others.

> *"I was raised to believe that excellence is the best deterrent to racism or sexism. And that's how I operate my life."*
>
> —Oprah Winfrey

According to some people, use of the term "bitch" has grown in direct proportion to the number of women who have reached the top of their field.

How do we get to the top of our field? We do our job very well, thus advancing to the next level. This usually requires that we work with other people, eventually being in charge of what those other people do.

An Inner Bitch Statistic:

There are 10.6 million women-owned businesses in the U.S. Some of them are sure to offer a nice selection of gift items, just in case you're shopping today.

If we ask those who report to us to do their job well, and that means they have to work harder than they did before, they will probably call us bitch.

If those people who report to us do not do their job and we take them to task for that, they will call us bitch.

"If being an egomaniac means I believe in what I do...then in that respect you can call me that. I believe in what I do, and I'll say it."

—John Lennon

Your Inner Bitch thinks he was talking about being a bitch, too.

If we have taken those people to task and they still do not do their job, we will undoubtedly be more firm with them the second time we talk to them. They will definitely call us bitch.

Good for them. Better for us.

Because what it really means is that we know our business. Here is a simple truth: No matter how nicely we ask, if we are the boss, we are the bitch.

What's the important part of that homily? We are the boss.

"We die by comfort and
live by conflict."

~

—May Sarton

Chapter Ten
Close
Encounters

t's bound to happen. And although it might sound to the uninitiated like a potential cataclysm, an encounter between two of us who are in touch with our Inner Bitch actually holds the possibility of greatness.

What could be better, after all, than the Inner Bitch doubled? Or tripled, quadrupled, increased exponentially? A close encounter with another Inner Bitch is always a good thing, because it keeps us sharp and can save us from spiraling into Toxic Niceness.

Your Inner Bitch wants you to plan a girls' night out for this Friday. Come on, you've got time to get those Bitches together in one spot, sitting around talking, eating, laughing, and getting to the bottom of things.

Consider this: When two of us in touch with our Inner Bitch meet head on, it's magnetic. We either feel ourselves drawn to each other or we are repelled. Either way, the dynamic that's going on is this: We're recognizing each other's power.

> "Several men I can think of are as capable, as smart, as funny, as compassionate, and as confused—as remarkable you might say—as most women."
>
> —Jane Howard
>
> *Think about it...*

We may not ever become friends with those women whose Inner Bitch we encounter, but that's beside the point. The important thing is, even if we have to agree to disagree, even if we just can't believe the tactics the other woman is using, even if we are filled with envy or some other base emotion, nine times out of ten, the other woman's Inner Bitch will evoke our respect and admiration.

It's better to recognize that confrontation can be exhilarating, that the process of facing off with someone who is as sure of her point of view as you are sure of yours is an opportunity to become more clear. A close encounter with someone's else's Inner Bitch is nothing to fear, it's something to welcome.

Your Inner Bitch wants you to reconsider competition. Think about what one actress said: "I am happy I have competition. It keeps me on my toes all the while and stops me from becoming complacent."

—Amisha Patel

Perhaps most importantly, there is the potential for great vitality in those interactions where our Inner Bitch meets Her match. It's easy to be with people who agree with us; it's comfortable and dulls our edges. This can be dangerous: Getting along with everyone in our lives gets to be a habit again, and Play Nicely gets a grip on us, beginning the spiral back into Toxic Niceness. Next thing we know, we're apologizing for everything, sitting home on Saturday nights waiting for the phone to ring, and eating the entire cake.

Is this what we want?

I don't think so.

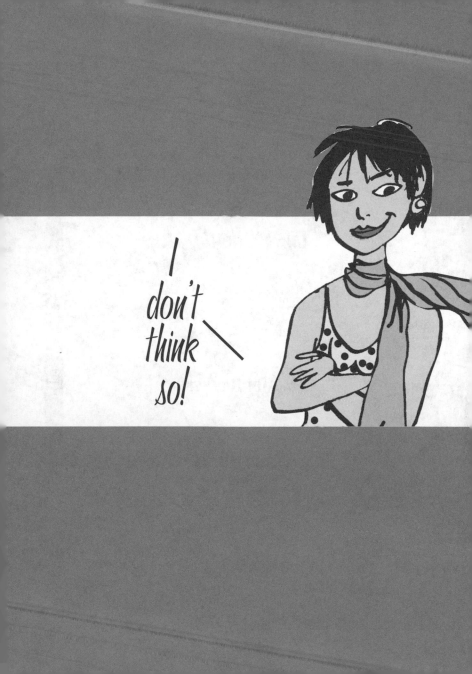

*"I am in the world
to change the world."*

—**Muriel Rukeyser**

Appendix A
The Bitch in Everywoman

The Inner Bitch manifests herself in many archetypes. At different moments, your own Inner Bitch may resemble any one of these icons of female power:

KARA

The Valkyrie swan queen. Kara overwhelmed her enemies using only the sound of her voice. A bitch to be reckoned with, especially on the phone. She also tells it like it is to her best friends.

LILITH

Lilith was to be Adam's first wife, but she took one look at him and said, "I don't think so." So off she flew to the banks of the Red Sea, where she spent her days coupling with whomever pleased her, giving birth to hundreds of children every day. Needless to say, with that level of fecundity, some of Lilith's DNA has got to be coursing through each of us.

CATHERINE DE MEDICI

When she married one of those Kings Louis of France, Catherine brought eighteen of her favorite Italian cooks with her. Can you imagine the leftovers? And her home was her castle: She insisted everyone at court use forks to pick up their food, instead of using their fingers. Yes, Mom.

KATHARINE HEPBURN

I refer here to the public persona, not the private person who slept on the floor outside Spencer Tracey's room. Strong, sassy, and ultra-dignified. Never knew that women were supposed to be the inferior sex. Next time you encounter a nasty salesperson, be Katharine Hepburn.

LYSISTRATA

A well-known Greek organizer. Persuaded the women of her city-state to withhold sex until the men gave up their most ridiculous war. The key here is that Lys banded together with other like-minded women. Imagine what we could do with the U.S. Congress...

To bolster your courage as you express that power-packed phrase, "I don't think so," call upon any one of these great role models, any time.

"Men and women are a lot alike in certain situations. Like when they're both on fire, they're exactly alike."

—Dave Atell

Appendix B
...And the Men Who Love Her

Just for the record, the idea that we women who are in touch with our Inner Bitch hate men, or wish we were men, or want to be like men, can be summed up with one word—SILLY. I just had to make that point.

This chapter is dedicated to the men who really admire the women they know who are in touch with their Inner Bitch. We all know men like this—they usually live with our friends. Oh, okay, maybe you actually live with a man like this. I do.

The point is, there's a name for men like this—Prince (as in, "a Prince among men"). This is not Prince Charming we're talking about here because your Inner Bitch knows that a Prince understands what the Inner Bitch is all about. He gets it.

Prince Charming is a myth—just like the unicorn. And your Inner Bitch wants you to stop believing in him.

A Prince Is Not A Wimp

Wimps are those guys who believe that machismo is the highest manifestation of male energy. They are the men who stand us up. The guys who keep dropping the age limit on whom they'll date, until their daughters and their girlfriends are the same age. The guys who won't work for a female boss. The guys who make us want to actually take the low road and share thoughts like:

"Sure God created man before woman. But then you always make a rough draft before the final masterpiece."

—Author Unknown

In the immortal words of the sadly-fictional Karen Walker: "It's funny because it's true...." But I digress. Back to the Princes of the world.

A Prince is a real man, i.e., a real human being.

Who Is A Prince?

Here's how to recognize a Prince:

* A Prince really does take full responsibility for his share of raising the kids;

* A Prince understands why those ads for beer are offensive (you know the ones I mean);

* A Prince never takes it for granted that we'll do all the cooking;

* A Prince does not assume that we can't change a flat tire;

* A Prince offers encouragement, rather than advice;

* A Prince knows what he knows. And, at the same time, he knows what he doesn't know. He doesn't bluster his way through a situation with ever-deepening b.s. In fact, a Prince has a good grasp on just how attractive it really is to be able to say, "I don't know."

Where Did He Come From?

Well, if we have an Inner Bitch who is a natural part of us, it must follow that there is also an Inner Prince.

Just as most women have been trained in the ways of Toxic Niceness, men have been trained in the ways of whatever it is they're suffering from. There are plenty of names for it; pick one. Chances are, if you've done your Inner Bitch homework, you won't need to be cruel about it. The point is to understand the dynamic at work here: Men have been taught behaviors that probably run counter to their true natures.

Nature vs. Nurture

My experience has been that it takes a lot of work for a man to become a Prince, but that the basic stuff is there all along.

And try this one on for size: Even the wimpiest, most macho man has the capacity to become a Prince.

Assessing The Prince Quotient (PQ)

I used to think that men were going to take the following test themselves. Now I understand that we must administer the test ourselves, preferably at an early stage in a relationship. A word of caution, however: don't try to do this during any major sports event, right before you leave for a party or family gathering, just after making love, too early in the morning, too late at night, too soon after getting home from work...all of which leaves a window of opportunity starting at about 12:30 on Saturday afternoon and ending at 12:45 the same day. Here goes:

1. Women like to be called "girls."
   Agree/Disagree

2. When a woman is assertive, I think of her as a bitch.
   Agree/Disagree

3. When I am going somewhere with a woman in a car, I drive.
   Always/Most of the time/Seldom/Some of the time/ Whose car are we taking?

4. I know how to do laundry and iron.
   True/False/Why bother? My mom does my laundry.

5. I had an emotional reaction to the movie Field of Dreams.
   True/False/Never saw it

Interpreting The Answers

Question 1

If you answered "Agree" and you are under the age of 65, it's a safe bet that you are not a full-fledged Prince. (-10 points, seniors get a 0)

However, if you based your answer on the fact that your mom and her friends like to be called girls, this reveals a level of sensitivity that implies Princeness. (+2 points)

If you answered "Disagree," take a moment to reflect on why you chose that response. Is it because women have corrected you for calling them girls? (+2 points)

Or was your answer based on thoughts you've had about the importance of language, and calling women girls is not only inaccurate, but insulting? (+10 points)

Question 2

If you agreed, define "assertive." (-10 points if your definitions for men and women are different)

If you disagreed take + 10 points.

Question 3

"Whose car is it?" is the question a Prince would ask. (+ 10)

"Seldom" indicates Princeness only if you own a car. (+ 7 if you own a car, -10 if you don't)

"Some of the time" seems equitable. (+ 5)

"Most of the time" may imply that you either drive a large car (conducive to carrying many people or things), or that you have a great car that everyone wants to ride in. (0 points) It may also mean that most of your friends don't own cars. Then you are generous to always drive them around, and we hope your friends pay for gas. (+ 10)

If your answer was "Always," we really do have to look at the reasons why that would be the case. But it doesn't look good for your Prince Quotient. (-10)

Question 4

Okay, this was a sort of trick question, and we won't add or subtract any points for it; I actually don't know how to do laundry. And I'm hopeless at ironing. We threw this on in to see if anyone was paying attention. Of course, if you're in junior high and your mom does all your laundry, that's just fine. No matter what answer you gave, take 0 points.

Question 5

Another trick question—everyone had an emotional reaction to that movie! "Emotional reaction," after all, covers quite a lot of territory. (0 points; it doesn't matter if you cried or not.) If you didn't see it, you are excused and may take an extra 2 points.

SCORING:

- If your score was 32 points, you are a full-blown, totally-in-touch Prince.
- If your score was 29, you have a high PQ.
- 19-21 is medium range PQ.
- A score of -32 shows a very low PQ. The fact that you took this quiz, however, is a hopeful sign, because awareness is the first step. Don't despair, there is no such thing as a hopeless case. You can improve your PQ.

Getting In Touch With Your Inner Prince

All the things in this book that apply to women getting in touch with our Inner Bitch also apply to men becoming a Prince. To break it down for you:

1. When you sense b.s., don't explain it away—call it as you see it. Even (or maybe particularly) when it is your own b.s.

2. If the desire to act like a wimp (see above) is overwhelming, just say to yourself, "I don't think so. Get a grip, fella." This works very well, because it bears a striking resemblance to taking the time to respond carefully.

3. Learn the difference between being kind and being patronizing. For example, it is kind to say, "May I help?" when you see someone struggling to get something done. Like putting two small children to bed. It is patronizing to say "Y'know, when I put them to bed, I just tuck them in and turn out the light."

4. Turn up the volume on your internal Prince voice. It's been there all along, whispering to you things like, "It really is okay to want to spend time with my kids."

Note:
A father spending time with his kids is parenting, not baby-sitting.

---

5. Recognize that your Inner Prince and my Inner Bitch meet on solid and very even ground.

Solid, even ground is a terrific base upon which to build.

"In the long run, we shape our lives,
and we shape ourselves.
The process never ends until we die.
And the choices we make
are ultimately our own responsibility."

—Eleanor Roosevelt

Appendix C
The 10-Minute Bitch

*T*here are little things we can do during the day to sharpen reflexes dulled by immersion in Toxic Niceness. As is the case with any sort of exercise, the more we do them, the easier they are. Consider these to be basic training. An Inner Bitch Reminder: When you give yourself the freedom to say "no," saying "yes" becomes more meaningful.

The Eye-to-Eye Exercise

Stand before a mirror and look yourself in the eye. Think of the last time someone requested something of you that was absurd. For most of us, that would have been within the past 24 hours. Something really silly, like the time your cousin went to India for a month for intensive meditation and asked you to feed her cats every day. In spite of the fact that this required you to drive for an hour, you said yes, didn't you?

Imagine she is asking you to do it again. Hear her voice, see her face. Now smile and say, "I don't think so, Cousin Menakshi."

This is especially instructive, because as you remember these absurd requests (whether or not you agreed to them), a pattern may become clear to you. These are the areas where Toxic Niceness is particularly strong in your life. This is important information to have, because awareness is the first step in eradicating unwelcome behaviors.

Voting With Our Pocketbooks

"Advertisers in general bear a large part of the responsibility for the deep feelings of inadequacy that drive women to psychiatrists, pills, or the bottle."

—Marya Mannes, *But Will It Sell?*

Gather together every magazine you have lying around the house. Go through them page by page and rip out any advertisement that offends you. You don't have to justify your being offended, just recognize it. Once you have all those pages gathered (there will probably be a large pile), make a list of the companies behind them and send them an email telling them you won't buy their products until they stop using offensive ads. Then follow through—don't buy their products. Do we want to give those companies our money? I don't think so. Eventually, they will get the message.

I Love Myself;
I Think I'm Grand

"Any transition serious enough to alter your definition of self will require not just small adjustments in your way of living and thinking, but a full-on metamorphosis."

—Martha Beck

You know those diet books and articles that you've accumulated over the years?

Destroy them. Each day, rip out a few pages to burn in the sink as you say, "I am an adult. I choose what I eat." If you don't think you look great, choose to take reasonable action. We all have enough information about how our bodies work; use whatever works for you. Most important, just say "I don't think so" to the unrealistic ideal everyone else sets for us. Women are supposed to look like people, not scarecrows.

Ten Most Wanted

Make a list of all the people who have taken advantage of your immersion in Toxic Niceness. It doesn't matter if they were manipulative, malicious, or mean-spirited, because their behavior is not the point. Yours is. Once a week, pick one of those people and outline for yourself the situation that occurred with that person.

Now, write it the way you wish it had happened, paying specific attention to your behavior. Don't be afraid; no one else is ever going to see this. The point is this: By rewriting our personal history, we are able to change our present and our future. Knowing what we wish we had done in a situation prepares us for the next time. And there is always a next time.

Your Inner Bitch knows that when faced with a situation that kicks you into High Toxicity, it's time to call a friend who can coach you out of it.

Coach One Another

This can be done in person, over the phone, by email, however it works for you. When faced with a situation that kicks you into High Toxicity, reach out to your Inner Bitch Coach as soon as possible. Explain the situation and ask for guidance. Because our friends want what's best for us and can usually see our lives more clearly than we can, they will be able to coach us back to the Inner Bitch way of doing things. For example, here's how some friends of mine used coaching to get one of them out of situation Toxic Niceness had gotten her into:

Friend A: "My coworker has been taking the train to work every day, which takes over an hour, and then she has to take the bus from the station to the office, which adds a half hour. I offered her a ride, so she's been taking the train to the station in my town and I drive us both to work. The problem is, she's a talker and conversation is the last thing I want in the morning. Plus, she shows up at my desk at the same time every evening, with her coat on and says, 'Ready?' I just can't take it anymore. I love my commuting time, it's the only time I have completely to myself. What do I tell her?"

Friend B: "Tell her your situation has changed and you won't be able to drive her to work any more."

Friend A: "What if she asks what's changed?"

Friend B: "Tell her you'd really rather not get in to that. Because the truth is, what's changed is your realization that you want that time to yourself and you don't have to explain that to anyone."

The Power Lullaby

I don't know about you, but the time I spend in bed just before sleep has always been a time of reflection for me. It used to work this way: I'd lie there thinking about all the awful things I'd done, starting when I was in pre-school. And I'd beat myself up about those things. In fact, I'd get so upset with myself that I couldn't fall asleep for hours, because one thing led to another and by the time I was drained enough to fall asleep, it was time to get up. Needless to say, I wasn't at my best.

I believe I have found a better way to deal with this reflective time. I think about all the things I have done right in my life. All those times I paid attention to my

Inner Bitch, and the times I've pulled myself out of a spiral into Toxic Niceness. I fall asleep with a smile on my face. And when I wake up in the morning, I feel powerful.

The truth is, we all—regardless of our history, regardless of what was possible or impossible yesterday— have only this day, this time, this place to begin to change. And each of us has the choice of what we will take from the banquet of life.

About the Author

Elizabeth Hilts lives in Connecticut, where she continues to evolve and grow in her bitchiness.

Since the first edition of *Getting in Touch with Your Inner Bitch* was published, Elizabeth has had the opportunity to share her experience and views with women (and men) all around the world. One of her proudest moments was learning that Rush Limbaugh had dubbed her a "radical feminist theorist," a title she is considering adding to her business card.

Elizabeth would like to see this book reach every woman who wants to laugh out loud and speak her mind.